SPLIT SECOND

SPLIT SECOND

Dennis McIntyre

Nelson Doubleday Inc., Garden City, New York

To John McDonald

Originally produced on the New York stage by John McDonald and Gus Fleming, SPLIT SECOND opened at the INTAR II Theatre on February 15, 1984. The cast was as follows:

WILLIS	*Bill Cwikowski*
VAL JOHNSON	*John Danelle*
PARKER	*Helmar Augustus Cooper*
CHARLIE	*Peter Jay Fernandez*
ALEA JOHNSON	*Michele Shay*
RUSTY JOHNSON	*Norman Matlock*

Directed by Samuel P. Barton
Scenery by Daniel Proett
Lighting by Leo Gambacorta
Costumes by Judy Dearing
Original Music by Jimmy Owens
Production Stage Manager, Dwight R.B. Cook

The production was transferred to Theatre Four on June 7, 1984 where it was produced by Philip Rose, Gus Fleming and John McDonald in cooperation with The Negro Ensemble Co. Inc.

CAST OF CHARACTERS *(in order of speaking)*:

    VAL JOHNSON
    WILLIAM H. WILLIS
    PARKER
    CHARLIE
    ALEA JOHNSON
    RUSTY JOHNSON

SETTING:
New York City. Manhattan.

TIME:
The present. The action of the play begins on the evening of July Fourth and ends on the morning of July sixth.

SET:
A continuous flow of action, set on various platforms, with suggestions of time and place, suggestions of New York City (Manhattan), and minimum props.

MUSIC:
The music should be comparable to the sound of wind chimes, tinkling, almost trembling. Its effect should be mysterious, haunting, and melancholy.

act one

ACT I

Scene 1

(Darkness. Music. Music out—gradually. Sound—labored breathing, running, building and building)

VAL: *(In the darkness—out of breath)* Freeze, motherfucker!

(Lights—night, a platform, a New York City side street, Twenty-eighth and Eleventh Avenue. Val Johnson, a black New York City cop, street clothes, and William H. Willis, white, street clothes. Val stands Upstage, breathing hard, his service revolver drawn, holding it with both hands, pointing it at Willis. Willis stands farther Downstage, panting, gasping for breath, slowly raising his hands. Willis starts to turn around)

VAL: I said, freeze it! You move, you even sweat, and you're wasted, pal! You want two more seconds of light, start staring at the green Caddie! Don't take your mind off it! Start thinking about the fucking ride, shithead! Just pretend I'm not here! *(Willis turns back and stares straight ahead, still trying to catch his breath. Val moves toward Willis)* Man, you should have been more picky. Going to jail for an Oldsmobile, now that's dumb, real stupid. You didn't even have to grow up to do that, did you?

WILLIS: *(Starts to turn around again)* Look—

VAL: I said freeze, fucker, you ever want to blink again! You'd better keep your eyes on that green Caddie! I'd do that, if I

3

were you, I really would! I'd start thinking about horsepower! I'd start thinking about chrome! That's what I'd do! I wouldn't want to make two mistakes in one night! No, I wouldn't want to do that, not with me behind you!

WILLIS: *(Turns back and stares straight ahead)* I mean, is this really necessary?

VAL: *(Moving closer to Willis)* Uh, huh.

WILLIS: Can't we, like, talk it over?

VAL: *(Closer to Willis)* Nope.

WILLIS: Have a heart, would you? It's the Fourth of July, for Christ's sake!

VAL: *(Right behind Willis)* Just another night to me, fucker.

(Val, his service revolver at his hip, pushes Willis forward and kicks his legs apart)

WILLIS: *(As it happens)* You don't got to do that, do you?

VAL: You want to bet?

WILLIS: Just where in the hell am I going to go? Tell me that.

VAL: That's the point, asshole. *(Begins to frisk Willis)*

WILLIS: I'm clean. Really. Hey, be a little more careful, would you? I'm a citizen.

VAL: *(Taking a large pocketknife out of Willis's right jacket pocket)* I'll keep that in mind.

WILLIS: You'd better keep that in mind, man.

(Val puts the knife in a jacket pocket. He takes a wallet out of Willis's right back pocket, opens it, quickly checks the identification, and then puts the wallet in a jacket pocket. He removes his handcuffs from his belt and snaps them on Willis, one at a time)

VAL: *(As he removes them)* Left hand!

WILLIS: *(As his left hand is cuffed)* I got an explanation. I do. I can explain. You got it all wrong. I wasn't messing with the Olds. I got an explanation. Really.

VAL: Right hand!

WILLIS: *(As his right hand is cuffed)* You don't need cuffs. I'm stranded, man. This is Eleventh Avenue. I'm not going anyplace. The last cab I saw, it was two days ago. You got to go to Eighth, you want a subway. I couldn't make it to Eighth, not with you chasing me. I'm out of shape. You know that.

(Val backs away from Willis. He holsters his service revolver. He removes a card from a pocket)

VAL: *(Reads from the Miranda card)* You have the right to remain silent. You are not required to say anything to us at any time or to answer any questions. Anything you say can be used against you in court.

WILLIS: What do you think? I don't go to the movies? This is fucking out-of-sight, man! You know that? It was my cousin's car. Really.

VAL: *(Replacing the card in his pocket)* We'll talk about it. As soon as we call your cousin.

WILLIS: He gave me the keys. He got a ride out to the Shore.

VAL: It must be nice, the Shore. I mean, if you live around here.

WILLIS: Look, he didn't need his car. I had his keys. Honest.

5

VAL: What'd you do? Drop them?

WILLIS: Yeah, that's right. They must have fell out of my hand.

VAL: I'm real sorry about that.

WILLIS: I had them. I did. I didn't know who the fuck you were. You scared the shit out of me.

VAL: You didn't even see me.

WILLIS: Right. I'll admit that. You guys are fast. Real fast. I know that. But I heard you. That was enough. This is a shit neighborhood. I mean, I told my cousin to get a garage. I told him I'd split it with him. I use his car a lot.

VAL: Real generous, your cousin.

WILLIS: He is. He's terrific. You should meet him.

VAL: *(Taking out his two-way radio)* I won't be here. You know, when he gets back from the Shore. *(Transmitting)* Officer Johnson. Holding one. Request transportation. West Twenty-eighth Street, off Eleventh. "500" block.

(The two-way radio crackles a reply)

WILLIS: A fucking Oldsmobile?! Jesus Christ, man! We could have talked things out! *(Turns around)* We still can— You? One of you guys?! Shit, no wonder I didn't see you!

VAL: Surprise.

WILLIS: Look, now we can talk. What do you say? We can make a deal. Fuckin' A, all this time, I thought you were white. You got a white voice, you know that?

VAL: No deal.

6

WILLIS: And you're not that dark either. Really. The right light, sunset, real early in the morning, you put a hat on your head, shit, man, no kidding, you could have come over on the fucking *Mayflower*.

VAL: You want to shove it back up your ass?

WILLIS: I was trying to compliment you, that's all I was trying to do. Ever since I was a kid, I've tried to concentrate on the positive aspects of life. You know what I mean?

VAL: You're not going anywhere. Concentrate on that.

WILLIS: All the crime in this fucking city, and we're talking about a fucked-up car. I'll bet there's three throats being slit, just while we're standing here. That's the kind of action you should be jumping on. A lot of people, they'd be real grateful not having their throats slit. Look, man, be realistic. What'd I do? I mean, really, brother? It was a '77 Oldsmobile. Nobody misses a fucking Oldsmobile, not in this neighborhood. They left it there to lose it. I would have been doing the city a favor. You know how much it costs to tow away a piece of fucking junk like that? Of course you do. You do it. Or your pals do. Shit, the muffler was hanging out all over the street. "Spark city," brother, that's all it was. What if the guy'd tried to pass one of those propane trucks? We'd be missing twenty blocks. There would have been fingers and toes in Connecticut. And there was a puddle of oil, maybe ten feet. I'm lucky I didn't kill myself.

VAL: You are.

WILLIS: I mean, talking about an abortion. Two of the tires were skinny, and the other two needed air. One of them had seven patches on it. I've never seen seven patches on a tire. That's why I counted them. The doors were open, brother, all four of them. I don't mean unlocked. I mean OPEN. The guy was just begging me to cart it away. If he knew who I was, he probably would have sent me the registration.

VAL: We'll check it out. See what he feels about it. How's that sound?

WILLIS: Check it out? You got to speak Spanish, you want to check it out. That was a spic buggy if I ever saw one. It had Jesus doing pushups on the rear-view mirror. It had fifty-two Virgin Marys all over the dashboard, for Christ's sake! If he'd had room, it would have had a palm tree! You don't want to take me in over a spic buggy. Not you. I mean, do you? Really?

VAL: No law against decorating your dashboard.

WILLIS: You couldn't see to drive it. There's got to be a fucking law.

VAL: It was parked. Remember?

WILLIS: I don't understand it. I really don't understand it. You know what?

VAL: What's that?

WILLIS: You got no sense of fair play. That's one thing you don't have, brother. *(Gestures)* Now, if I'd been fiddling around with the Caddie over there, you might have had ample cause. It's an '81. It's got respect written all over it. *(Spells it)* R-e-s-p-e-c-t! But an Olds, a '77 goddamn Olds—that's a one-night stand, brother. You get up the next morning, you wouldn't even wipe your ass with it.

VAL: You're a real pisser, aren't you?

WILLIS: No, see, it's like this, I'm the black sheep in the family. No offense there, bro, but I've been in trouble before. You're going to find out. You've got computers. I know that. But it's all been small stuff. Nothing big. Like the Olds. That's my style. I don't beat up grandmothers, man. I don't rip off purses. I don't even own a gold chain. I never took heroin in my life. I don't even know what the shit looks like. Somebody

8

offers me coke, I turn it down. That knife, it's for my protec-
tion. It's a tough city. You can understand that. You carry a
gun, don't you? Look at my fucking wardrobe. People don't
dress like this, not when they're in the money. I mean, do I
look like I'm part of the cash flow? Do I look like crime pays?
(Looks down at his suit) This is one step above Woolworth's.
The spics are breathing down my neck. They're starting to
dress better than me. That car, that heap, that was to buy a
new suit. So I could go to court. So I could look decent. So I
could make a favorable impression. My ex, she's breaking my
balls. Alimony. Child support. You might appreciate that. I've
been around black chicks. Marlene, my ex, she's just like a lot
of black chicks. Gorgeous in bed, real nifty, you know what I
mean, right? But one step away from the sheets, all of a sudden, she's putting a bat between your legs, just for fucking
practice.

VAL: *(Low)* You're not helping your case.

WILLIS: Look, brother—

VAL: *(Low—dangerous)* Don't call me fucking brother.

WILLIS: What else am I supposed to call you? You and me, we're
in the same category.

VAL: The fuck we are!

WILLIS: No, listen, we're deprived, that's all I'm saying. Eco-
nomically deprived. We always have been—always will be. My
father was a prick. Yours just happened to be colored, right?
(Val flinches—visibly) Look, you get me to a phone booth.
One block over. It's not busted. Twenty-ninth. Back on
Tenth. I'll give you a number. You dial it, there's a thousand
bucks waiting. All you've got to do is dial 846-5745—No—It's
896-5745. My brother's place. He's got a large insomniac
problem. He's always up late. He owns two dry cleaners. He
keeps a lot of cash in his house. He doesn't trust the night
deposit. A thousand bucks, brother! It's cheaper than bail.

That's why he'll pay it. It's happened before. He always pays my bail, my brother—and then he screams at me. What do you say? *(Val stares at Willis—hard—and shakes his head "no")* Hell, it's the Fourth of July, man! Have a heart. I got kids. Two girls. Six and ten. Real cute— *(Val continues to stare at Willis)* All right, then let's talk about your twelve fucking kids, nigger! How's that?!

VAL: *(Dangerous)* I'd be real quiet, if I were you. Real quiet.

WILLIS: Got you there, didn't I? Finally touched a nerve, right? I was beginning to think you didn't have no emotion, bro. Now, your kiddies, I'll bet they could use a couple thousand real fresh bucks, couldn't they? I mean, you could probably spring at least six of them. You know, fix it up with the prosecutor, as long as he's got big lips and frizzy hair, right? You got a wife on the side, brother? A couple thousand bucks, you and the little lady, you could get *(Intentional dialect)* "yourselves" a lifetime supply of penicillin, couldn't you? Why don't you give your foxy bitch a call? See what she thinks about it. You don't want to do that? No, I wouldn't want to do that either. Not this late. I wouldn't want to disturb her, not when her mouth's full. Or how about a two-thousand-buck transistor radio? I'll bet you've already got a hard-on just thinking about it. Five hundred fucking stations, man! Wouldn't be nobody but nobody riding the subways no more, would they? And I'll even throw in a pair of earphones. Free. No extra charge. Just call it a jigaboo bonus. How's that grab you? Wait a minute. One more thing. A real package deal. Six-foot shoes. Gold and orange. No, excuse me. Make those roller skates. Purple and green. Concentrate, brother! Get a fix on it! A 125th Street, Saturday night, and you'd be the heaviest fucking dude stomping the pavement!

(Val stares at the street, his body rigid, trying to control himself)

VAL: You keep talking, asshole, and you won't even be able to fucking limp!

WILLIS: Is that a fucking fact?!

VAL: That's a fucking fact!

WILLIS: What's wrong, bro? You don't want to talk to a white man? You don't want to negotiate? William H. Willis, he's not good enough for you? No dope, no deal? No pussy, no action? *(Val takes a step toward Willis, but then stops. He stares down at the street again)* Fucking nigger cops! How'd you get the job, anyway? Suck off another fucking spearchucker cop?! That's what they call progress, don't they? They ought to take all you nigger cops and ship you back to Africa. That's what they ought to do. Let you be jungle cops. Give you some beads and a spear. Let you direct traffic in the jungle. Because that's where you belong, nigger! Didn't you know that?! I mean, like don't you miss the smell of elephant shit?! *(Val slowly removes his service revolver. He points the revolver at Willis, his arm trembling. Willis laughs—moves closer—a bravado)* Just try it! Go on! See where it fucking gets you! *(Val continues to point his revolver at Willis, and then slowly holsters it)* You don't got the balls, do you? Well, I can understand that. Really. Most niggers, they only come with one ball, that's what I hear. *(Moves slightly closer)* Hey, I got a joke for you. You want to hear a joke? What's the difference between a nigger cop and a pile of shit? No difference, man! Get it?!

(Val draws his service revolver, points it at Willis, and pulls the trigger. An explosion from the revolver. Willis is thrown backward. He sags to the ground, jerks, and then lies still. Val replaces his revolver in his holster, turns away from Willis, takes several steps, and then stops. He turns back, stumbles to Willis, searches in his own pockets for the handcuff key, finds it, unlocks the handcuffs, locks them again, replaces them on his belt, takes out Willis's knife, opens it, wipes with his jacket, puts the knife in Willis's right hand, and then begins to back away. He remembers the wallet. He takes it out, wipes it on his jacket, moves back to Willis, and puts it in Willis's back pocket. He backs away again, panting, taking deep breaths. He removes his service revolver and begins moving Upstage. Blackout)

Scene 2

(Music out. Lights—another platform. A New York City Police Precinct, an office, later that evening. Parker, a black police captain, studies Val's report. Val sits. He sips from a cardboard container of coffee)

PARKER: Nice. Real clean. I'd say just about textbook. Right down the line.

VAL: What?

PARKER: *(Taps the report)* One shot. That's all it took. You're not reckless. Not you, Johnson. Not when it comes to ammunition. Usually, it takes two shots. You know, one for good luck. Especially when it's dark. Especially when it's around Twenty-eighth and Eleventh. Some of those guys, they can be fierce. It's a good policy—squeeze off two—if you're going to squeeze off anything. But you, Christ, you're some shot. You drilled him right through the heart. The perfect shot, Johnson. Hell, the guys up in sharpshooting couldn't have done it better. Practice a lot?

VAL: I used to.

PARKER: When was that?

VAL: When I was a kid.

PARKER: Pittsburgh. You grew up in Pittsburgh, right?

VAL: That's right.

PARKER: A lot of crime in Pittsburgh.

VAL: A lot of crime here.

PARKER: *(Taps the report)* I can see that. Real serious crime, too. But we're keeping ahead of it, aren't we? Or, at least we're trying to keep ahead of it. Pittsburgh? You really had a gun in those days?

VAL: I had two guns.

PARKER: Two guns? What kind?

VAL: A thirty-eight and a twenty-two Magnum.

PARKER: Some people, they just get born into the right family, don't they? Shit, I couldn't even talk my old man into a BB pistol. I had to settle for cap guns, but my mother kept hiding the caps on me. I always got shot first. That didn't make it too much fun.

VAL: Parker, I'm tired. I'm not getting paid for this, I'm off duty, and I've got a wife I haven't even called.

PARKER: No, you're not getting paid for this, you should have called your wife, and I'd rather be out at Rockaway taking a stroll along the beach. But we've got to get the facts straight, don't we? Or, at least sorted out.

VAL: *(Indicating the report)* See the blanks? They're all filled out. There isn't anything else.

PARKER: Well, there must be something else. There might just be something else. Usually, there is something else. Otherwise, I wouldn't be the investigating officer, and there wouldn't be a Departmental Hearing Friday morning, would there?

VAL: It just might be that he was white.

PARKER: It just might be. And it just might be that it's official police policy. I wonder what he was doing that far downtown —a guy from Queens. A white guy from Queens.

VAL: He was trying to steal a tan, '77 Oldsmobile. *(Points)* Line seven, in case you missed it.

PARKER: *(Stares at the report)* You've got real legible handwriting. That's a good trait. Every little bit helps when you're a cop, doesn't it? What color cars did they have in Pittsburgh? Black-and-whites?

VAL: Black-and-whites. What's the point?

PARKER: Good combination, black-and-white. We never should have dropped them. A lot more mystery, black-and-white. Green-and-white—blue-and-white—it makes crime too colorful. The same thing happened when the Department issued blue pens.

VAL: I remember. It was real traumatic. But I thought we were talking about a tan, '77 Oldsmobile.

PARKER: See, the thing that bothers me, Johnson, most guys, most officers, they never have to go through it once. You know, wasting some dude. Most guys, most officers, they go thirty years, and it gets rusty in their holster. But if it does happen, if they have to take it out, it usually takes them awhile to get over it. And the first night, that's the worst night, even if the pincushion was a real scumbag. But you, it just seems to me, you don't give a flying fuck about what you just did. I mean, let's be realistic, Johnson, you just reduced the population by one.

VAL: He tried to kill me. What am I supposed to feel?

PARKER: Well, I guess it's no fun feeling mortal for a couple of seconds, is it? You get used to life, don't you? And I guess everybody reacts differently. Three feet, right?

VAL: Three feet.

PARKER: Look, I've got to ask. It's blocking my thoughts. How'd you ever get a permit in Pittsburgh?

VAL: You mean, how did one of us folks get a permit in Pittsburgh?

PARKER: I'm interested in the permit, that's all.

VAL: Really?

PARKER: Look at my skin.

VAL: Sweet.

PARKER: See, what I'm getting at, it was a little difficult on 110th, if not impossible, unless you knew somebody. Especially in those days. And nobody spoke much English, so I was out of my element.

VAL: My old man was a cop. He fixed it.

PARKER: Sweet. Kind of a family tradition?

VAL: He likes to think of it that way.

PARKER: You and your old man, you did a lot of shooting together?

VAL: Weekends.

PARKER: You win any prizes?

VAL: I'm not interested in prizes.

PARKER: No?

VAL: No.

PARKER: That must be true. This guy, Willis, he wasn't much of a prize. Arrested fourteen times, three convictions, small stuff. Never attacked anybody. Didn't seem to be the killer type—

VAL: I saw his sheet.

PARKER: Looked up his background?

VAL: That's right. Wouldn't you?

PARKER: I'd probably do that. It's nice to know the facts after the fact, isn't it? Nope, he wasn't any prize. I don't think too many people are going to miss him. Maybe his brother in Queens. The guy owns two dry cleaners. You'd think he would have given him a job sorting hangers or something. Kept him off the streets. And his mother, she might miss him. He had a mother in Detroit.

VAL: I know that. And his father died in 1957, four years after Willis was born. First stretch, Jackson Prison, arrested in Lansing. He tried to hold up a Dunkin' Donut, figured it'd be a lifelong career, so he decided to come to New York. I'm tired.

PARKER: Okay, okay, just a few more things. Christ, imagine if it was Berkowitz instead of this cat Willis. Or Chapman. What a prize! How come you called for a radio car before you cuffed him?

VAL: I didn't cuff him.

PARKER: That's right. I forgot. You didn't get a chance to cuff him. I hate nights. My mind wanders. All the details get lost. I've been thinking about a Virginia ham on whole wheat for the last five minutes. Maybe a couple of pickles. Why didn't you just call in when you spotted him jerking around with the Olds?

VAL: I figured I could handle it. It was one-on-one.

PARKER: Johnson, most cops in this city, me included, you call transportation when you've got the cat laced over a hood. Not when he's just waiting around for you to make a move. Christ, don't you ever watch television?

VAL: I had him covered. He looked docile.

PARKER: A lot of sweet-faced kids, give them a chance, and they'll take your ears home with them. Didn't your old man ever tell you that?

VAL: I chased him three blocks. He was out of shape. I didn't think he'd try anything.

PARKER: That's the trouble with being on the street too much— you begin to think you own it. Procedure doesn't mean shit when it's one-on-one time, right? That's what I like about being in the office. You can't fuck up that much. Throw away one piece of paper, you've still got five more. Three feet?

VAL: *(Indicating the report)* That's what it says, doesn't it?

PARKER: Sure it does. That's how I know. How's your coffee?

VAL: I'd like to sleep.

PARKER: Wouldn't we all? If I didn't have a wife, two kids, a mother-in-law, and a Buick, shit, I'd never get up. I heard you were in Vietnam. Is that true?

VAL: You looked it up. Why ask?

PARKER: I don't believe everything I read. When was it?

VAL: Most of '68. The spring of '69.

PARKER: How was it? Intense?

VAL: Sometimes.

PARKER: You guys, you vets, you call it Nam, don't you?

VAL: That's what we called it over there.

PARKER: Sounds strange, Nam. Sounds like half a country.

VAL: It was.

PARKER: You take a lot of risks?

VAL: What's that got to do with William H. Willis?

PARKER: I'd just like to know, that's all.

VAL: I did "point." You were paid to take risks.

PARKER: A scout?

VAL: Something like that.

PARKER: What'd you do? Volunteer?

VAL: That's right.

PARKER: How come?

VAL: We kept running into snipers. I thought I could do something about it.

PARKER: Did you?

VAL: Nobody got hit for five months.

PARKER: You must have been good.

VAL: It kept me alive.

PARKER: That's real dangerous work—being the "point man."

VAL: It could be.

PARKER: What about close calls?

VAL: What about them?

PARKER: Did you have any?

VAL: I didn't go looking for close calls.

PARKER: So, most of the time, you were careful, right?

VAL: I was always careful.

PARKER: Five months—you didn't take a lot of chances.

VAL: I didn't take any chances.

PARKER: Don't go out in the rain, you don't get wet?

VAL: I just didn't want to be last in line holding my medals.

PARKER: Sure, I can understand that. It's who you know that counts. And whether or not he's white. But I still don't get it, Johnson. You're careful over there. You don't fuck around. Not once. But you come back here—

VAL: I was a target over there.

PARKER: You could have been a target tonight.

VAL: I didn't have forty guys depending on me. It was a collar. I've done it a hundred times, so I took him on solo. This time he got stupid, real stupid, so he ended up dead. That's all we're talking about, Parker—logical progression—stupid to dead. He pulled the knife, so I pulled the trigger. Nothing else applies.

PARKER: You do much killing in Vietnam?

VAL: No.

PARKER: Come on. Not even one?

VAL: If I did, I didn't see him.

PARKER: It gets real easy to kill when you can't see them. I read a book on the subject. Two books.

VAL: Parker, I just shot a car thief who was coming at me with a knife. There's a six-thousand-mile difference. What do you say? Why don't we just stick to that?

PARKER: Look, I'm just trying to make an analogy.

VAL: Stretch it, it won't fit. So why don't we just drop it?

PARKER: No, let me finish, see if it gets us anywhere. I don't get homicides on a regular basis.

VAL: He had a knife. Remember?

PARKER: That's right, he did. That's why I never went into Law. I just couldn't get the terms straight. Homicide, suicide—all the "cides" began to sound the same. Anyway, the point I was trying to make, the analogy, it's real dark in the jungle, isn't it?

VAL: So what?

PARKER: I'm not trying to be an expert, Johnson. I've never been in a jungle. I don't even like walking in the woods. But I've seen enough movies about us folks to get a pretty good idea of what a jungle looks like. Real dark. Even in the daytime. All those trees growing into each other for centuries. And I remember reading something about Vietnam, or maybe I saw it on TV. Guys in the jungle, they used to empty out two hundred rounds if they even heard a twig snap. Three hundred rounds if a fly landed on a branch.

VAL: They had rules about that.

PARKER: Well, we can't enforce all the rules, can we? Now, it seems to me, it's awfully dark on Twenty-ninth and—

VAL: Twenty-eighth.

PARKER: That's right, excuse me, Twenty-eighth. Awfully dark, there, too, being so close to Twenty-ninth. And real deserted, too.

VAL: It wasn't that dark.

PARKER: Not like the jungle?

VAL: Not like the jungle.

PARKER: Well, you were there. You ought to know. I just saw the movies.

VAL: And there was a streetlamp on Twenty-eighth.

PARKER: Busted. That's what they told me.

VAL: It wasn't busted two hours ago.

PARKER: You didn't happen to shoot it out, did you? No, one shot, right? I keep thinking there should have been two. Maybe somebody busted it after you left. Shit, they're all busted up there. You'd think they'd turn off the electricity. Save money. It's too bad "warning shots" went out. You might have scared him. Still, two verbal warnings . . . Some guys, they just don't listen, do they? Three feet? You really got that close?

VAL: I got that close.

PARKER: I never liked getting close. That's why I decided to get off the street. That and my mother-in-law. I just couldn't get used to touching guys I didn't know. Some cops—they really enjoy slamming a guy into a wall. That might even be the reason they join up. But not me. You were patting him down, right?

VAL: It never got that far.

PARKER: You had him spread out, didn't you?

VAL: It never got that far either.

PARKER: He just turned around, three feet, knife out?

VAL: He turned around, one foot, knife coming out. I backed up two.

PARKER: He must have been desperate.

VAL: He must have been.

PARKER: And that's when you warned him?

VAL: I told him to drop it. That was his second warning. The first warning, I told him to freeze.

PARKER: Let me get this straight. He had his knife out, he was coming at you, and you had time to warn him.

VAL: "Drop it" doesn't take a whole lot of time.

PARKER: Well, it's a good thing you didn't say, "Drop that fucking knife, you cocksucking bastard, or I'll put a bullet through your miserable heart!" *(Parker moves to Val, turns away, and counts off three feet. As he does so)* One. Two. Three. *(Turns his head behind him)* Let's go through it one more time, okay?

VAL: *(Not moving)* This is bullshit, Parker.

PARKER: Look, it'll save time on Friday. *(Val slowly faces Parker's back. Parker sticks his pen in his belt)* Get rid of your coffee cup. You weren't drinking coffee, were you? *(Val sets his coffee container on the floor)* Good. Now, point your finger at me. We don't want to get too realistic.

VAL: People pay us for this?

PARKER: Go on. Point. I just want to figure something out. *(Val pauses, and then raises his finger, pointing it at Parker's back. Without looking)* You pointing at me?

VAL: I'm pointing at you.

(Parker, the pen suddenly in his left hand, wheels around and has it against Val's throat in two seconds. They stare at each other)

PARKER: I'm surprised he didn't cut off your balls, Johnson.

VAL: He's dead, isn't he?

PARKER: *(Lowering the pen)* I didn't see your finger move.

VAL: Neither did he. And he had it in his right hand.

PARKER: Yes, he did. The quality of observation, that's a nice quality to have in police work. But three feet, his height, your height, and given the fact, most cutters, they come in real low —what I'd really like to know, Johnson—what baffles the living fuck out of me—how'd you ever pump one into his heart? I mean, you should have pulled it off in his face, or, at least put it through his neck.

24

VAL: He wasn't very good with a knife, he didn't come in low, and he was trying to open it.

PARKER: It's real sad. They get sloppy, a lot of those guys. They stop practicing, don't they? Well, at least it was quick for William H. Willis.

VAL: He didn't go out humming, if that's what you mean.

PARKER: They usually don't. Too many other things to think about. Con Ed bills. Laundry. Season tickets.

VAL: Is that it?

PARKER: I was doing a tour, playground on Seventy-second, tried to break up a fight. This Mexican kid came at me with an ice pick. He came in real low. That kid kept in shape. Right for my belly. Fast. He must have been in training for ten years. I caught him twice. Once in the nose, once in the right cheek. But, see, I had time to aim. I was standing nine feet away from the punk. That kid, that Mex, he had it in for me. He would have cut out my heart and stuck it in his mother's enchilada. But the funny thing, the really strange thing, you'd think I would have forgotten about him. Chalked him up to good shooting. But I haven't. And I had the right to do it.

VAL: So did I.

PARKER: I hope so, Johnson. Unless you get nicked in the line of duty, you're going to be around for a long time.

(They stare at each other. Blackout. Music)

Scene 3

(Music out. Lights—another platform. A bar. A short time later. Val and Charlie, a black cop, street clothes, sit across from each other at a table, each drinking a mug of beer)

CHARLIE: He was ripe, Val. You didn't have any other choice. You couldn't cuff him. He pulled a blade. You're a cop. What'd he think you were going to do? Sharpen it for him? What'd he expect? I'll bet he went down looking real surprised. They always do. Dumb—some of those mothers—fucking dumb. They go along real cool, then it gets hot out one night, or their old lady won't twist it for them, and they fucking lose it. *(He leans across the table in an attempt to unzip Val's jacket. As he does so)* Hey, man, it's July. At least unzip it.

(Val pulls away from Charlie—slightly. They stare at each other)

VAL: Air-conditioning, Charlie—I get colds from air-conditioning.

CHARLIE: Sure, I can understand that. I get pneumonia swimming at Jones Beach in February. Look, it's over. The guy'd been in and out of shithouses—what?—since he was a kid. You did us all a favor. If it hadn't been you, it might have been me. Or Fleming. Or Carlos. He was a mark, Val. He was wearing a card on his heart. I don't get it. They walk around just inviting us to put a hole in them. We all know that. And then, when we finally do it, we're fucking depressed. Beats

27

me. *(Charlie sips his beer and studies Val)* Look, a mother-fucker's a motherfucker, no matter who started throwing him against the wall when he was six months old. And once a motherfucker, always a motherfucker, dead or alive. It was up close, that's all. If you'd shot him off a roof, you'd be home in bed asleep. *(Val nods)* Val, it's a well-known fact in the Department that nobody but nobody digs close-up work. It looks great in the movies, but, shit, who in the fuck wants to sniff a Big Mac and fries just before some freak gets taken out? You want to know about "up close"? I was talking to this guy in Burglary—Johnny Williams. Some dude on Canal Street came at him with a cleaver. It took five shots to put him away, and this dude was still swinging on number four. Now that's up close! Drink your beer. Let it go, man. The creep was a flea. Just like the dude on Canal. A dog wouldn't have pissed on either of them. *(Val nods and sips his beer)* You call Alea yet?

VAL: It doesn't work over the phone.

CHARLIE: That's what I'm doing here, right?

VAL: Right.

CHARLIE: My advice—and it's worked wonders in the past—get a leave. Get out of the city. Don't start hashing it around here. Take a couple of days—drive—relax. I'll tell you one thing—you sure as hell bagged that son of a bitch the right time of the month. Christ, I hate this weather. It means I must be civilized or something. The ancestors—they used to have lunch on the equator. *(Charlie studies Val)* Val, would you stop fingering that glass? It drives me crazy. I can't concentrate. I keep waiting for it to break. That's why I can't stand drinking with Carlos anymore. That's all he ever does—all night—fingers his glass and comments on the diameters of every good-looking ass comes in the door. No self-control—Carlos. I don't know how they ever gave him a badge, let alone a gun, and you're starting to be his replacement.

VAL: This guy—Willis—he was white.

CHARLIE: He could have been black, Puerto Rican, or American Indian, for all I care. He pulled more than two inches on you. He took more than one step. If he was looking for a souvenir, well, he sure as hell got it. You've got the license. He didn't have one. You remember that. If that dude'd waltzed in my direction, I would have emptied out on him. Shit, I'd still be clicking away. I'd get real nervous knowing I might not be able to get it up anymore. Real nervous.

VAL: I keep thinking, Charlie—

CHARLIE: That's not a good trait. Not right now.

VAL: I keep thinking—if he'd been black—maybe I wouldn't have shot him.

CHARLIE: What do you mean you wouldn't have shot him? That's what they trained you to do. The color doesn't mean shit. Fleming's old man, he shot two dudes. Both black. He said he didn't know what color they were until they were dead.

VAL: I don't remember doing it, Charlie. Really doing it. Pulling the trigger. I was starting to walk away—all of a sudden, he was on the ground—I don't even think I heard the shot . . .

CHARLIE: That's the best way to remember it—you don't re-member it. You've got other people to worry about. Alea, the old man, me— *(Shakes Val's shoulder)* Come on. I'll buy you another beer. We'll talk about all the good things we're going to do.

(Charlie picks up the beer mugs and exits)

VAL: I had him cuffed, Charlie . . . *(Val puts his elbows on the table and leans his head against his hands)* I had him cuffed.

(Slow blackout. Music)

Scene 4

(Music out. Lights—another platform. Val and Alea's apartment. A short time later. Val enters the apartment. Alea is asleep on the couch. He takes off his jacket. He takes off his holster and service revolver. He moves to her and sits down beside her. He runs a hand through her hair—very tenderly. She slowly wakes up. She slowly hugs him)

ALEA: What time is it?

VAL: Four. A little after.

ALEA: Four? *(Rubs her eyes)* Did something happen?

VAL: It was busy, that's all. I did overtime. *(Gestures at the door)* You forgot to lock the police bar.

ALEA: *(Slowly sitting up)* I thought you'd be back earlier. I dropped Rusty off—what?—ten-thirty? I bought him a beer. He liked the fireworks.

VAL: *(Gestures at the door)* I'm going to put a sign up—"Bolt me."

ALEA: I'll remember. Is it really four o'clock? I didn't mean to fall asleep here—

VAL: Anybody could jimmy the lock. He doesn't even have to be good.

ALEA: I'll remember. I promise.

VAL: Second time this week.

ALEA: I'm half-awake. Quit scolding. It's four o'clock, and I've got a class in five hours.

VAL: How'd you like to skip it?

ALEA: I'd like to, but I can't.

VAL: Why not?

ALEA: I've already been out twice.

VAL: We could drive upstate. Look at some land for Rusty.

ALEA: They did homework. I'm supposed to collect it.

VAL: We could find a place, have dinner, take our time—

ALEA: You've got to work tomorrow night.

VAL: I'll get Charlie to cover. Or Carlos. They're both off tomorrow. They owe me.

ALEA: We can do it Sunday.

VAL: No, tomorrow's better.

ALEA: We've got the weekend.

VAL: I need to get out of the city.

ALEA: But why tomorrow?

VAL: *(Pulls at his shirt)* How come you didn't turn on the air conditioner?

32

ALEA: I fell asleep, that's all.

VAL: It's got to be eighty-five—ninety degrees in here.

ALEA: Val?

(He moves away from her)

VAL: I had a close call tonight.

ALEA: *(Slowly sits up)* What happened?

VAL: Some punk pulled a knife on me.

ALEA: A knife?

VAL: He dropped it.

ALEA: Where'd it happen?

VAL: Twenty-eighth and Eleventh.

ALEA: Was it a kid?

VAL: A kid, right. Eighteen, nineteen. I'm not sure.

ALEA: How big was the knife?

VAL: Big enough.

ALEA: What kind of knife was it?

VAL: Kitchen.

ALEA: Did he try to use it?

VAL: He made a move. But he wasn't that fast. He was high. We found a bunch of "shit" on him.

ALEA: Eighteen years old?

VAL: Something like that.

ALEA: Those bastards!

VAL: Right.

ALEA: Was he black?

VAL: Black, right—

ALEA: He had a knife. I guess it doesn't matter, does it?

VAL: No—

(She moves to him. She embraces him)

ALEA: Why don't we stay overnight?

VAL: We can't. I mean, I can't. *(Moving away)* I've got to be back Friday—

ALEA: I'll take Friday off, too. We'll come back late.

VAL: I've got a meeting. Friday morning.

ALEA: What kind of meeting?

VAL: Routine. Departmental.

ALEA: What time?

VAL: I've got to be back, that's all. It's early. Ten o'clock.

ALEA: I don't remember any Friday morning meetings.

VAL: I've been skipping them. Captain sent me a memo. "I'm missed"—that's what it said. I don't want to push it.

ALEA: Then we'll come back tomorrow night. Do you want anything to eat? Some tea? *(He stares straight ahead. He shakes his head "no")* Val?

VAL: I'm telling you, the next punk who comes at me with a knife—the next punk who comes at me with anything, I'm going to pull the trigger!

ALEA: What?

VAL: *(Faces her)* I'm getting to hate it. I don't know, you knock down one jerk, four more stand up behind him.

ALEA: He really scared you, didn't he?

VAL: He didn't scare me. I wanted to tear him apart. I almost did— No, forget it. It's over.

ALEA: Why didn't you call?

VAL: I went out for a beer. I ran into Charlie—

ALEA: Charlie?

VAL: Right.

ALEA: Charlie's been working days.

VAL: He was looking for some action. He came around.

ALEA: Was it more than just a kid with a knife?

VAL: No, it was a kid with a knife, that's all. One night's worse than another. The Fourth of July—it's always nuts. It was just another incident. I should have called—

ALEA: How serious was it?

VAL: Look, I don't want to talk about it right now. Really. I just don't want to go through it again. I want to get some sleep. I want to get out of this city. It'll blow over. Like it always does. Like it has to. It was automatic. It was reflexes.

ALEA: What was?

VAL: This guy—what happened—

ALEA: I thought it was a kid. A black kid.

VAL: All right, it was a kid!

ALEA: Who do I have to ask? Charlie? He's got the details, doesn't he?

VAL: Some of them.

ALEA: Who else are you going to tell? Rusty?

VAL: Look, I survive. That's all you've got to know. Sometimes I get home late. Sometimes I forget to call. That's it.

ALEA: That's it?!

VAL: That's it! That's enough.

ALEA: People talk about their jobs!

VAL: I talk about my job.

ALEA: I get the anecdotes. I get the laughs. That's your style.

VAL: The rest is ugly. The rest stays on the streets.

ALEA: You live here. I have a right to know.

VAL: I didn't marry you so I could tell you goddamn cop stories all night!

ALEA: No? Then what am I supposed to think about while you're gone?

VAL: You've got your kids. You've got your classes. Why mix it up with a lot of shit?!

ALEA: Then what am I supposed to think about while you're here? You don't want me to know anything about your work, except that one night's dangerous, one night's not.

VAL: You got it!

ALEA: How am I supposed to know which night is which?!

VAL: You're not supposed to know!

ALEA: Then what do you need me around for?! You come home three hours late. You don't call. But I'm not supposed to say anything. I'm not supposed to ask questions, because, no, we don't talk about your work.

VAL: Alea, leave it alone.

ALEA: We talk about my work instead, don't we? My school. The kids. Do they like me? How come they don't like me? What's so goddamn important about teaching English when they'd rather speak Spanish? But let's forget about you. Let's leave the Police Department out of it. That's the way you want it, isn't it?

VAL: That's the way I want it, yes!

ALEA: Because you've always got to be in control, right?

VAL: You lose it, you let it go for a second, you even snap your fingers, somebody else picks it up, and fast!

ALEA: Is that what your father taught you? Is that Rusty's code?

VAL: No, it's mine. I learned it early—starting at six—starting in Pittsburgh. I got dragged off the Hill. I got tied to a tree. I got my clothes ripped off with a knife. I got poison ivy rubbed all over me. I hung there for five hours. It got dark out. I was still there. That's when I learned it.

ALEA: You were six years old, Val.

VAL: It could have been yesterday.

ALEA: And so nothing else counts?

VAL: Not a fucking thing!

ALEA: Nothing else defines you, right?

VAL: It got me through a war, and it gets me through my job!

ALEA: And what's it do to me, Val? *(He turns away from her)* What's it do to you?

VAL: *(Without looking)* Let it go.

ALEA: Why?

VAL: Because you wouldn't like to hear about this one. Not this one.

ALEA: No? I'm supposed to be a partner, remember? I don't give a good goddamn if Rusty never told your mother anything. All I know is that I'm tired of watching fifty percent of you disappear every night when you come through that door, barred or not barred, and I'm tired of knowing that fifty percent of me can't function when you're around me.

VAL: You wouldn't want to hear about this one.

ALEA: Why not?

Peter Jay Fernandez, John Danelle

John Danelle, Michele Shay

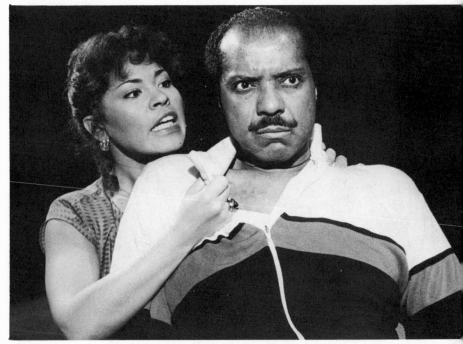

Michele Shay, Norman Matlock

VAL: Nobody wants to hear about this one.

ALEA: Try me.

VAL: You don't want to hear about it!

ALEA: Try me!

VAL: All right. Why not? Let's get you involved in my job.

ALEA: Don't make fun of me.

VAL: The Fourth of July. A big night in my life. I offed a white dude. Twenty-eighth and Eleventh. I put him out of commission for good. One shot. Right through the heart.

ALEA: Oh, my God, Val.

VAL: You wanted to know, didn't you?

ALEA: I wanted to help. I want to help.

VAL: Help? No way you can do that, baby. Morgue van picked him up four hours ago. William H. Willis. Very white. Numbers and burglary. Out of Detroit. A ten-page sheet on him. Two stretches in New York. Sing Sing and Riker's. This time it was a car. A '77 Oldsmobile. He tried to snatch it. I wasn't on a break. Unlucky for me. Unlucky for him. I happened to spot him first, and now he's laid out, courtesy of the city, Thirtieth and First, waiting for his brother.

ALEA: Why . . . Why'd you shoot him? Val?

VAL: The shit pulled a knife on me, that's why! So I blew his fucking chest away! How's that sound?! Three feet away from me! No time for conversation! No time for manners! He was dead with his stomach in his mouth before he even hit the street! Hey, maybe you should have been there!

ALEA: Val!

VAL: Quite a sight, baby! Real involvement. A cop's wife, right beside him. Action. Frontline action. You could have chalked him, told your kids about it, spent a whole lesson drawing it on the blackboard—

ALEA: It was self-defense!

VAL: Sure it was. Of course it was. But you still should have seen it. I mean, not much up front—just a neat round hole—but check out his back, no shoulder blade. But you're right. A clear-cut case of self-defense. A cop's life on the line. A black cop's life on the line, but still a cop. I've got the badge, he had the knife, and, white or not, did that son of a bitch ever look surprised when the last thing he ever saw was the look on my face!

ALEA: Val? That's not the way it happened, is it?

(Val turns away from her. He shakes his head "no")

VAL: I had an hour left. If he'd tried to steal it an hour later, I could have looked the other way. I could have done that. I didn't need to chase him. It was a goddamn car, falling apart. He wasn't even driving it. But I had to make it important. I had to do my job. I couldn't let him get away.

ALEA: How'd it happen?

VAL: *(Faces her)* I had the cuffs on him. I was waiting for a radio car. I was standing seven, maybe eight feet away from him. I had my gun on him. "Procedure" to the letter. I heard the siren. I guess I must have jumped. It was dark. There weren't any streetlamps around. Firecrackers were going off all over the place. I accidentally pulled the trigger.

ALEA: What about the handcuffs?

VAL: I had time. I took them off.

ALEA: What about the knife?

VAL: He had a knife. I opened it. I wiped off the prints. I stuck it in his hand.

(Alea moves to him. She embraces him)

ALEA: Then there's nothing to worry about—is there?

VAL: No . . .

(The lights begin to fade to darkness. Music. Blackout. Music out)

END OF ACT ONE

act two

ACT II
Scene 1

(Darkness. Music. Music out—gradually. Sound—a television set —a police program—the volume barely audible. Lights—another platform. Rusty Johnson's apartment. The living room. The next evening. Rusty sits in a leather armchair watching the television [not seen]—a can of beer in one hand—a remote control in the other hand. He is dressed casually. He wears a pair of fancy cowboy boots. Val enters—a change of clothes—but still casual.)

RUSTY: *(Watching the television program)* Shh. *(Val sits down and watches the television program—no interest in it)* Do you believe that horseshit? Just strolls in. The door isn't even locked. Whatever happened to stakeouts? *(To Val)* Ever notice how the black dude always trots in second? You think they're trying to tell us something? The guys who write these shows, they ought to do a tour, find out a few things. They ought to make it mandatory. *(He pushes a button on the remote control—snaps off the television)* What are you doing out tonight, son? I thought you were working.

VAL: The Fourth—I did overtime. I got the night off.

RUSTY: How was it last night? Jumping?

VAL: I was downtown. Nothing special.

RUSTY: I always hated holidays.

45

VAL: I know.

RUSTY: New Year's Eve, I'd start punching people out at eight and keep on punching till four. Did I ever tell you? I used to put lead in my gloves.

VAL: No.

RUSTY: It saved a lot of time. You want a beer?

VAL: No. *(Gestures)* How's the leg?

RUSTY: *(Pats his left leg)* Coming along. Just picked up a new pair of stirrups. Won't happen again. No more tumbles. Never should have bought cheap stirrups. Cutting corners, that's all I was doing. But it was a fifty-buck difference, and I had my eye on that Mexican saddle.

VAL: I would have bought it for you.

RUSTY: I like picking up my own accessories.

VAL: I remember. You made Father's Day tough.

RUSTY: Pick them up yourself, nobody can throw them back in your face. *(Pats his left leg)* No, it wasn't Stallion's fault. Cheap stirrups, that's what did it.

VAL: Aren't you ever going to name that horse?

RUSTY: Stallion's fine. That's what he is, isn't he? Just taught him two more words last week. I'd like to see the bastard tries to steal that horse. Better be fluent in German, or he's going to find his ass wrapped around a couple of trees.

VAL: There aren't too many German horse thieves around anymore, Dad.

RUSTY: You never can tell. A lot of people, they end up surprising you. There was this loony in Pittsburgh. I used to arrest him all the time. Every other month. Larry Malone. Worst thief you ever saw. Incompetent. So bad it was downright embarrassing. Usually pulled his heists when he was stewed. A brick-through-the-window type. Or, if he couldn't find a brick, a garbage can. I picked him up one night. He was carrying a twenty-one-inch Admiral portable. Right down Forbes. Three in the morning. A streetcar almost hit him. We saved his goddamn life. Anyway, we got him in the black-and-white, stashed the portable—you remember that portable—it was in your grandmother's house . . .

VAL: Right.

RUSTY: Worked real well, that Admiral. Your grandmother never had any trouble with it. Where was I? Larry Malone, right. *(He studies Val)* What are you doing here, son?

VAL: I had an incident last night.

RUSTY: What kind of an incident?

VAL: I shot a guy.

RUSTY: Dead?

VAL: Dead.

RUSTY: First time outside the Army?

VAL: I didn't kill anybody in Nam.

RUSTY: Funny. You know, I always assumed you did. We never talked about it. I was always waiting for you to mention it, but you never did. A whole year, and you didn't shoot anybody?

VAL: I did "point." It didn't come up.

RUSTY: It's a real shame.

VAL: What?

RUSTY: All that free ammo, tons of it, and you didn't have anything to show for it.

VAL: Disappointed?

RUSTY: You've either got a target, or you don't. You know this guy you shot? Ever see him before?

VAL: No.

RUSTY: One of us?

VAL: White.

RUSTY: Well, that's one for our side, isn't it? He have a gun?

VAL: Yes.

RUSTY: Did he pull it on you? *(Val looks down. He nods "yes")* Did you have yours out?

VAL: *(Looks up)* Not at first.

RUSTY: You should have had it out. Fast draws went out a long time ago. *(Rusty studies him)* He was the first one, son. Not many guys are lucky enough to pull thirty-five years without having to face it.

VAL: No . . .

RUSTY: What do you mean, "no"?

VAL: That's not the way it went down.

RUSTY: What isn't?

VAL: I killed him.

RUSTY: Well, Christ, yes, you killed him. What else are you going to call it? He had a gun. It was pointed at you. You squeezed first, that's all. Justifiable homicide, that's what it's called.

VAL: He didn't have a gun.

RUSTY: What do you mean, "He didn't have a gun"?!

VAL: He didn't have one, that's all.

RUSTY: Then why in the hell did you tell me he did?! He had a knife, right?

VAL: He had a knife . . .

RUSTY: Knife can kill you too, in case you didn't know that. What'd he do? Come at you with it?

VAL: He had a knife in his pocket. I took it off him.

RUSTY: What kind of shit is this? No gun—no knife . . . He lunged at you, right? He made a quick move.

VAL: I had my gun on him . . . It accidentally went off . . .

RUSTY: Accidentally—accidentally went off?!

VAL: Yes!

RUSTY: Why in the hell didn't you just cuff the son of a bitch?!

VAL: I had a radio car coming. I didn't think I needed to.

RUSTY: You didn't think you needed to?! That's why they issue handcuffs! So you can put your gun away!

VAL: I know that!

RUSTY: You didn't know it last night!

VAL: I didn't want to get close.

RUSTY: They pay you to get close.

VAL: It didn't seem like he was going anywhere.

RUSTY: You made sure of that, didn't you?!

VAL: It was an accident!

RUSTY: You don't pull out a gun and have accidents. Kids have accidents with guns. There must have been some provocation. Something!

VAL: I can't remember . . .

RUSTY: What do you mean, you can't remember?! Did he look like he was going to scatter? Did he pick up a rock? Did he put a hand inside his coat?

VAL: He was yelling!

RUSTY: He was what?!

VAL: Yelling!

RUSTY: Yelling?! Shit, that's not against the law! They've got a right to yell! You're putting them away! Didn't you know that?! What were you doing last night? Drinking?

VAL: I wasn't drinking.

RUSTY: You should have had him cuffed! You don't put a bullet in somebody, no reason, except he was yelling at you, getting on your nerves! The worst cops I knew, the most they'd do, maybe break a kneecap—an elbow—

VAL: Look, I remember the stories. You and Lloyd, you both carried throwaways. Just in case you made a mistake.

RUSTY: That's right. But we never made a mistake.

VAL: What do you mean, you never made a mistake? You killed three guys! There had to be a mistake!

RUSTY: There wasn't any mistake! Not one! I had reason! Just cause! Provocation! All three times! Two of them had me on the ground, and the other son of a bitch was coming at me with a two-by-four!

VAL: So what?! You still carried throwaways! You kept the mistake in mind!

RUSTY: We all carried them. It was part of the ritual in those days. We used to pass them around in bars. But I only knew one cop who ever used it, and he got caught. Sure, we talked big. We carried throwaways. We had trick holsters. We had to. We were all scared shitless. But we didn't have accidents. Guns didn't just go off. People didn't die just because we got jumpy, nervous, distracted, or whatever you want to call it. So, don't start in on me, boy! You pulled the trigger! Not me! I didn't ask you to be a goddamn cop!

VAL: Didn't ask? What else was there? I grew up with cops. The only people who ever came over to our house were cops. Cops and cops' wives. Cops and cops' kids. And once in a while, a real distinction—some goddamn prosecutor who should have been a cop! I mean, traffic cops, vice cops, street cops, homicide—Lloyd, Frank, Daryll, every partner you ever had!

RUSTY: That's how I kept my job!

VAL: The hell it was! You loved it. Being a cop, that was special. The world couldn't get along without cops. In fact, cops ruled the world. That's how society functioned. I remember, Mom and me, we must have spent two thousand hours waiting for you to change your goddamn uniform. And where in the hell were you? Drinking your Rolling Rock with the boys, that's where you were. Cleaning your gun, loading it, unloading it—

RUSTY: It came in handy, my gun!

VAL: Sure, it did. But where in the hell were we, Mom and me? Out front, waiting, watching the hookers get booked. Or the guy who'd just carved up his wife with a screwdriver and then blown off his six-year-old daughter's head with a shotgun. Or the broad who'd just burned down her house, except her husband and four kids just happened to be in it. What are you talking about, you didn't ask me to be a cop?! I started being a cop at five. The first Christmas I can remember, under the tree, a fingerprint kit. A goddamn fingerprint kit. And a black-and-white, made out of tin, with your name painted on the hood, "Rusty," and the number of your squad car, "183." I broke it Christmas Day, winding it up, listening to the siren. My God, you had me in uniform when I was ten. All those precinct blasts in Oakland. Fake ribbons. Fake medals. All the ribbons and medals I was supposed to earn when I grew up. First in the Army, and then on the force. You got me a flasher for my bike. I was eleven years old, and I was arresting every other kid on the block!

RUSTY: It was my profession! What'd you expect?! We were living on the Hill. I was a black cop. That was something in those days—a black cop. I was proud of it. And, sure, I brought it home. What else was I supposed to bring home? What else was I supposed to do? Pretend I was a goddamn surgeon? Put clamps and a scalpel under the tree? Buy you a book on anatomy? No, I'm not going to listen to this! Why in the hell am I defending myself?! I'm not about to eat my gun just because you grew up in a cop's house! Just because you lost your cool last night! You're on trial, kiddo! Not me! Manslaughter, that's what you gave those bastards!

VAL: I didn't give them shit!

(Rusty studies Val)

RUSTY: I must be losing my edge. I didn't see it coming. You fixed it, didn't you?

VAL: I fixed it.

RUSTY: You planted the knife.

VAL: I planted the knife.

RUSTY: And that makes it a whole different story, doesn't it?

VAL: It makes it self-defense.

RUSTY: He came at you, right?

VAL: Right.

RUSTY: And you warned him.

VAL: I warned him twice.

RUSTY: Neat.

VAL: That's right. Neat.

RUSTY: No witnesses.

VAL: Nobody.

RUSTY: And that's it?

VAL: There's a departmental hearing. Tomorrow morning.

RUSTY: And you're going to lie again?

VAL: When are you going to realize—when are you going to learn—it's not our fucking world! When are you going to understand that?!

RUSTY: Then maybe you should have picked cotton for a living! There are rules!

VAL: Sure there are! White rules!

RUSTY: Rules, buddyboy!

VAL: And sometimes they apply, sometimes they don't, right?!

RUSTY: If you accept them, you live by them. Nobody's supposed to like you. But I still got through thirty-two years.

VAL: Thirty-two years, and you didn't even make sergeant. Fourteen citations, and you never saw a stripe.

RUSTY: That's right. But I'm alive. I've got a pension. I've got a disability. I've got everything they promised to give me. I get to ride a lot now. I could afford the move here. I could afford your mother's funeral. I can afford this apartment, and, one of these days, I'm going to nail down a piece of land. We're talking about police money. It got me through the Depression. It got your mother through the Depression. And when you came along, you had a roof over your head. You ate. You went to school.

VAL: Those were necessities!

RUSTY: I didn't expect anything else!

VAL: Dad, those were necessities! Everybody else took them for granted. Why in the hell do we have to be grateful?!

RUSTY: Times were different. I was grateful.

VAL: They aren't any different now. Who do you think is running this country? All of a sudden, they're setting us back fifty years. Why should I be grateful? Just because you were?

RUSTY: You listen to me! A cop back then, a black cop, they tossed him into Hazelwood. God dropped all his rejects in Hazelwood, and I took care of them. Me, Lloyd, Jackson, Frank, and a few other guys. And you didn't last long, not in that neighborhood, not if you were chickenshit. One sign of weakness, and they'd find you behind a garage, your throat slit, so wide they could see into your stomach. Or your head caved in, four slugs from your own gun. And do you think the Department cared? You want to know what it was like being a black cop in Pittsburgh? A nigger cop? It was the bottom of the ladder. No rungs, kiddo. You just hung on, that's all you did. You got base pay. No raises. No bonuses. No promotions. None. And if you even thought about opening your mouth, then you cleaned out your locker the same night. Don't tell me things haven't changed. You've got black captains today. If you thought you'd seen a black captain in Pittsburgh—1945— they would have put you in a tight jacket and hustled your ass out a side door!

VAL: Snails crawl faster than we do.

RUSTY: But they get there. They get there.

VAL: Sure, if somebody doesn't step on them.

RUSTY: The destination, that's all that counts.

VAL: We make it to the corner, we're lucky.

RUSTY: What's the alternative? Watts? Detroit? Where in the hell did they get us?

VAL: They got us noticed.

RUSTY: And last night? Where'd that get us?

VAL: I've done enough for them! I fought their goddamn war!

RUSTY: You couldn't even find a target. How'd that help?

VAL: You don't even have an idea, do you?

RUSTY: You wasted a lot of ammunition, that's all I know.

VAL: I had you in mind, half the time I was over there, and that's all you think? I wasted a lot of ammunition? One time —one time I got across a paddy on "point." But all of a sudden, it seemed wrong. "Charlie" was real close. All around me. He hadn't bought the bait. He'd let me get across. He knew what he had behind me. I couldn't get anybody on the radio, so I started back. I was doing a number on "Charlie's" trap, so I expected a bullet in the back. And the only thing that went through my mind, the one thought, waiting for that bullet: "What's Rusty going to think?" His son took a fucking bullet in the back. "What in the hell was he doing to get a bullet in the back?!" Just thinking about you, it must have made me run faster, because when "Charlie" finally squeezed, he missed me by ten feet. I didn't waste ammunition. I heard it coming at me—nine long months!

(Rusty turns away)

RUSTY: *(Without looking)* You never talked about it. You should have talked about it.

VAL: I didn't bring back any medals. What was I going to talk about?

(Rusty slowly turns back to him. They face each other)

RUSTY: So, what are you going to do about last night, son? Let it ride? *(Val looks away. He nods)* This guy you shot—you ever going to think about him?

VAL: *(Without looking)* No.

RUSTY: Then what'd you come around for? Absolution?

VAL: *(Faces Rusty)* Maybe. *(They stare at each other)* I'll give you a call.

RUSTY: *(Speaking with difficulty)* I don't want to hear from you, son. I'll read about it, or I won't hear anything at all.

(They continue to stare at each other)

VAL: *(Begins to exit)* I'll call you.

RUSTY: Val? *(Val faces Rusty)* If it'd been a black dude, this guy, would you have shot him?

VAL: The gun went off accidentally.

RUSTY: It's too bad.

VAL: What?

RUSTY: If we were still in Pittsburgh, I might have been able to help you.

VAL: I had him cuffed.

RUSTY: I thought so. I didn't think you were that dumb.

(Val exits. Music. The lights slowly fade on Rusty)

Scene 2

(Music out. Lights—Val and Alea's apartment. A short time later. Val enters the apartment. Alea, a change of clothes, waits for him. They stand apart. Alea studies him)

ALEA: What'd he say?

VAL: What I figured he'd say.

ALEA: He wants you to tell?

VAL: That's right.

ALEA: You're not considering it, are you? Are you?

VAL: The way it stands, it's a fucking mess.

ALEA: It was an accident, that's all it was.

VAL: It couldn't have been an accident. I had him handcuffed.

ALEA: It was an accident. Accept it.

VAL: It was right through the heart. That's not an accident.

ALEA: It happened to be right through the heart. You didn't aim.

VAL: I'm too good at it. That's what scares me. I'm a professional. I mean, I fought a war for a whole year. I had guns in my hands every day for a year, and I never had an accident.

ALEA: You're not perfect. That's Rusty's department.

VAL: If it was an accident, then why'd I take the cuffs off? Why'd I plant the knife? Why didn't I just leave it the way it was? Tell them what really happened. Dropped the "three feet." Dropped the "knife." Dropped the "warnings."

ALEA: There would have been too many complications, that's why. You knew that, so you rearranged it.

VAL: *(Shakes his head "no")* I fixed it. I remember fixing it.

ALEA: You altered the setting, that's all you did. You can live with that. So can I.

VAL: I tampered with evidence. That's a felony.

ALEA: I can live with that too. So can you.

VAL: That simple?

ALEA: It has to be that simple.

VAL: Rusty doesn't figure I can live with it.

ALEA: It never came up when he was a cop. He can afford to be righteous—he's got a horse to ride.

VAL: But I'd already called for a radio car. I didn't need to have my gun out.

ALEA: You were scared.

VAL: I wasn't that scared. He was eight, ten feet away. He was cuffed. He couldn't have done anything.

ALEA: You didn't know that. He could have had friends.

VAL: He was a loner. I spotted it right off.

ALEA: It was Eleventh Avenue. It was dark. It was late.

VAL: But why him? I've been alone, lots of times, worse streets, and I didn't need a gun in my hand—

ALEA: It was the Fourth. It was crazy out.

VAL: I've worked the Fourth before.

ALEA: But this time you were scared. It was security. You don't think Charlie wouldn't have had his gun out? Or Carlos?

VAL: I don't know.

ALEA: I've heard them talk.

VAL: But mine went off.

ALEA: And what if Charlie's had gone off? What if Charlie'd had him handcuffed? You don't think Charlie wouldn't have planted the knife? You don't think Charlie wouldn't have wiped off the fingerprints? Charlie would have done the same thing you did. Except Charlie would have walked away from it. Charlie would have justified it. Charlie would have turned it into a funky story. It would have been one night in Charlie's life, and he wouldn't have even thought about it the next day.

VAL: That's too easy.

ALEA: That's fact. That's reality, Val, and you know it.

VAL: I'm too good a cop. It never should have happened.

ALEA: That's Rusty talking, not you.

VAL: I'm still a good cop, and it still shouldn't have happened.

ALEA: My God, you're looking for an excuse to tell them, aren't you?

VAL: How am I supposed to go back out on the streets?

ALEA: It was settled! He came at you, three feet, knife out. It was self-defense. That's what you told them, and that's what they wrote down. You walked out of here tonight, you just wanted to talk to Rusty. You talked to him, and, all of a sudden, you're actually thinking about letting them know what really happened. And what if you did? Do you think they'd believe you?

VAL: I don't know.

ALEA: Do you?!

VAL: They might.

ALEA: Did Rusty? *(He turns away from her—for a moment)* What's the alternative? I don't plan on visiting you twice a month for the next ten years. There's too much at stake, Val. So, feel bad. Go ahead. Replay it in your mind, every minute, every day. Replay it to your advantage. Or don't. Think about it every time you're running after somebody on the street. Or stop running. Get a transfer. Do rescue work. Do desk work. Lock up your gun. Feel terrible. Feel dishonest. Feel like a coward. Feel like a cheat. But you're going to live with it, like it or not, and so am I. There is no decision to be made. It's made. It was made the day you were born—when you ended up black instead of white. It was made, Val!

(They stare at each other)

VAL: A guy like Willis, I always figured I'd be able to handle it. You know, skip the lies, tell the truth, fuck the consequences. I didn't know shit, did I?

ALEA: You're just not Rusty, that's all.

VAL: So what's that make me?

ALEA: You're alive, aren't you? Who cares about the truth anymore? Who ever did? Unless they got caught. What's the
truth mean, anyway? You recited his record. He was a pimp.
He was a hustler. He was a thief. He smuggled cigarettes from
North Carolina. He went to prison in New York. He went to
prison in Michigan. He carried a knife, and, if you'd given
him a chance, he probably would have killed you. That's your
fucking truth, Val. But he was white. Don't you ever forget
that. White! You tell them what really happened, and they'll
crucify you. And not just you. Me. All of us. The next black
man who wants to become a cop, you think they're not going
to think twice about giving him a gun? The next black kid
they blow away in Bed Sty, you don't think they're going to
bring up your name? Because when black people pull the trigger, that's not insanity, that's spontaneity! Give a gorilla a
banana, he's going to eat it! And I'll tell you one thing, Val
Johnson, you go to prison, you won't survive it. The guards are
going to hate you. You're the ex-cop who couldn't control
himself. The whites are going to hate you. You're the ex-black
cop who couldn't control himself. "Control," Val! Remember? But the blacks, they're going to hate you most of all. And
do you want to know why? Out of contempt, that's why!
Contempt! Why'd you have to go and let them know!

VAL: Then where in the hell are we?

ALEA: You tell me! But keep that in mind, tomorrow morning,
and keep asking yourself the other question—"Where are we
going to be?"!

*(They stare at each other—hard. He turns and exits the apart-
ment. The lights slowly fade on her as she stares after him. Music)*

Scene 3

(Music out. Lights—another platform. A park bench. A short time later. Charlie, a change of clothes, sits on the bench. He is sipping a beer, a paper bag around the can. A paper bag with another beer in it is set next to him. Val moves to the bench and sits down beside Charlie. Charlie hands him the paper bag. Val takes the can of beer out of the bag, opens it, and takes a sip. Charlie keeps glancing at Val. Val stares at the ground and keeps twisting the beer can in his hands)

CHARLIE: What's happening? *(Refers to Val's beer)* Better cover it up. Cop might come along. *(Charlie sips his beer. He watches Val twist the beer can in his hands)* What's up, man? You still got that asshole on your mind? *(Val nods)* It'll be a breeze. You'll be in and out in ten minutes. Don't eat. I'll buy you breakfast.

VAL: *(Looks up)* You ever kill anybody, Charlie? Nam? Here? I never asked you.

CHARLIE: Nam. Bach Ma. I got a guy up close, like you did, except I used a knife. He slipped under the wire—four satchel charges—a special delivery. It took two guys to get my hand off the handle. I must have been standing there, maybe twenty, thirty minutes, holding this "Charlie" up. My namesake. So, I know what you're going through, man. I've been there.

VAL: What about here?

CHARLIE: I haven't had the chance. But I haven't been looking for it either.

VAL: One "Charlie"? That's it? *(Charlie stares down at his beer. He drinks)* That's it?

CHARLIE: *(Looks up)* I knocked off a corporal. Saigon. White. A real prick, this guy. He was dealing scag, low-grade stock, the pits, skipping all the directions, lacing it— No, man, you don't want to hear this— *(Val stares at Charlie. Charlie sips his beer)* See, the word got around, guys were getting themselves into deep shit. Convulsions, that kind of stuff. One guy, brain damage. Another guy a kid from Alabama, real competent—a real good pool player. He OD'd on it. Threw himself out a window. Landed on a motorcycle. A lot of the black guys, this corporal, he was their contact. Sold it to them cheap. Maybe ten bucks. A big bag. Made it seem like you could get through a whole tour on one bag. The white dudes, the ones into the heavy stuff, this corporal, he took care of their bags, too. Except it was a hundred percent for them. Real Asian bliss. So, this dude, this corporal, he was dealing two bags. A white bag, and a black bag. And the "brothers" were getting "schizo," while the whites were off dreaming the good dream. Well, we decided to take him out, this corporal, and I got the low card. *(He sips his beer)*

VAL: How'd you do it?

CHARLIE: We grabbed him off the street. Two in the morning. He was making his rounds. We'd been following him for five hours.

VAL: You shot him? *(Charlie shakes his head "no")* Then what?

CHARLIE: You sure you want to hear this?

VAL: I want to hear it.

CHARLIE: Put a wire around his neck. The idea was—he should go out slow. And he did. I don't know what they did when they found him. We never heard anything. I don't think they gave him a Bronze Star. He had a reputation.

VAL: What if he'd been black, Charlie?

CHARLIE: Wouldn't have happened. Everybody takes care of their own. At least we did over there. You know that.

VAL: You didn't give him a chance?

CHARLIE: No, I didn't.

VAL: No explanation?

CHARLIE: None. We had the facts.

VAL: Murder?

CHARLIE: Euthanasia, that's what I like to call it. I lost maybe a night's sleep over it. The "Charlie" I gutted, he stayed with me a lot longer. But wasting that corporal, it saved a lot of black boys. It saved them a lot of pain.

VAL: It was still murder, Charlie.

CHARLIE: Look, man, what do you think?! The world runs on flowers?! He was dealing bad scag to the "brothers"—turning whites into fucking lotus blossoms! There comes a time you don't take it anymore! And that's not "murder one"! No way! That's just getting it on and doing what's right when everybody else is looking the other way! *(Someone passes in the park)* What are you staring at, shithead?!

VAL: You took him from behind. You didn't give him a chance.

CHARLIE: He didn't deserve a chance! Certain people, they don't belong here! They don't have the credentials! And that scum-

67

bag, he happened to be one of them! All right, it wasn't pretty. It wasn't neat. It wasn't by the book. It wasn't like your caper. He didn't have a knife on me. He wasn't coming at me. I didn't have to warn him. But he was a killer, baby, just like your customer! Except he didn't need a knife. He had a chemistry set, and you tell me, what's the fucking difference?! *(He stands. Squeezes the beer can and tosses it behind him)* I came out tonight—I figured you needed help. I figured I'd help you out!

VAL: I do need help.

CHARLIE: How come?

VAL: I need help, that's all . . .

CHARLIE: The dude from Detroit, it wasn't clean enough for you? He maybe should have stuck it in you a couple of times before you pulled the trigger? Is that what's bothering you?

VAL: It wasn't three feet . . .

CHARLIE: No?

VAL: It was nine feet—maybe ten—I wasn't close . . .

CHARLIE: Three feet, and you could dream at night, right?

VAL: Right!

CHARLIE: Shit, I would have smoked the motherfucker at fifteen feet—I even saw the tip of a blade!

VAL: But he wasn't—he wasn't—

CHARLIE: He wasn't what?!

VAL: I didn't—

CHARLIE: What are you talking about, man?

VAL: I didn't—I didn't have him cuffed . . .

CHARLIE: Let me get this straight. It wouldn't have happened, you had him cuffed. He couldn't have reached for his knife, right?

VAL: No!

CHARLIE: What do you mean "no"?!

VAL: That's not how it happened! I put it in him!

CHARLIE: You sure as shit did! The cat's dead!

VAL: I put it in him—cuffed!

(Val looks away. Charlie studies him)

CHARLIE: No knife coming out, right?

VAL: No knife.

CHARLIE: No fancy footwork. *(Val shakes his head "no")* But they don't know that, do they?

VAL: No.

CHARLIE: Then that makes us just about equals, doesn't it? *(Val looks up. They stare at each other)* How'd it go off?

VAL: The guy was a "lip," so I pulled it out. I figured it might impress him.

CHARLIE: You should have rapped on his neck. That's all it takes.

VAL: Radio car was around the corner. I didn't start out to mess him up.

CHARLIE: So you put a bullet in him instead?

VAL: It was an accident.

(They stare at each other. Charlie slowly nods)

CHARLIE: If that's what it was, then fuck them. It's "street." They don't know anything about it. And the less they know, the better. *(Charlie rubs Val's shoulder, but the affection is gone. As he does so)* But they've got a shovel for people like you. My advice—don't let the mothers use it. I left it in Saigon. No regrets.

VAL: Did you?

CHARLIE: You leave it on Twenty-eighth. You play good-guy cop, Johnson, you won't have a friend left in the world. Guaranteed. That's just the way it is, brother.

(Charlie exits. Music. Val stares straight ahead. The lights slowly fade on Val as he begins to walk away from the bench)

Scene 4

(Music out. Lights—Val and Alea's apartment. A short time later. Alea, no change of clothes, stands in the middle of the room.
Rusty—no change of clothes—approaches the platform. He stops. He stares at her—and then enters the room. They stare at one another—uncomfortably)

RUSTY: We could have talked about it over the phone.

ALEA: It's too easy over the phone.

RUSTY: It's his decision.

ALEA: He's your son. He needs your help.

RUSTY: It's still his decision.

ALEA: If you don't support him, he can't make it.

RUSTY: He knows what I think.

ALEA: And that's why he can't make it.

RUSTY: There's only one decision.

ALEA: In your mind.

RUSTY: In anybody's mind.

ALEA: He already told them one story.

RUSTY: I know.

ALEA: He can't tell them another one.

RUSTY: That's up to him. He took an oath.

ALEA: And he made a mistake.

RUSTY: That's why he took an oath.

ALEA: He changed things around, that's all he did.

RUSTY: That's a crime.

ALEA: And you wouldn't have done that, right?

RUSTY: I wouldn't have taken off the cuffs. I wouldn't have planted the knife. If it was an accident, it was an accident.

ALEA: No, you wouldn't have touched the handcuffs. You wouldn't have opened the knife. You were the perfect cop, weren't you?

RUSTY: I was a tough cop. I was a good cop.

ALEA: No, the Pittsburgh Police Department, they threw away the mold the day you retired. That's what you like to think, isn't it?

RUSTY: I like to think I did a decent job. I like to think I was fair. There were some rough neighborhoods.

ALEA: But cops today, Val included, they're all second-rate, aren't they?

RUSTY: It depends.

ALEA: On what? How they stack up against you? No, you wouldn't have accidentally pulled the trigger. You weren't capable of shooting a man in handcuffs, were you? That was beyond you, wasn't it?

RUSTY: I was capable. Just like Val.

ALEA: Sure you were. But you're a bit more special, aren't you?

RUSTY: No. I just never did it. I never had the "accident."

ALEA: But it never would have come up, right?

RUSTY: No, I don't think it ever would have come up.

ALEA: There wasn't even a possibility, was there?

RUSTY: There was always a possibility. I just kept it in check, that's all.

ALEA: And that's why you can be so calm. That's why it's so easy for you to pass judgment, walk out of here, feed your horses, and start jumping fences!

RUSTY: It's not easy!

ALEA: No?! In case you didn't know it, Rusty, it's our life! It's the next ten years! The next twenty!

RUSTY: I know that.

ALEA: No, you don't! You're quoting scripture, that's all you're doing! You could be talking to anybody. Take a goddamn look! I'm your son's wife! Val could go to jail, and you could be dead before he got out! That's what you're promoting! He's your son! Where's your compassion?!

RUSTY: You don't want compassion! You want approval!

73

ALEA: No, I don't want interference! Your interference! I don't care if Val took off the handcuffs! I don't care if he planted the knife! We don't owe them anything! Nothing!

RUSTY: No, we don't, if we don't want to. But I don't see how that's going to improve anything.

ALEA: I'm not interested in improvement! I'm interested in Val!

RUSTY: Val joined the Police Department! He took an oath! He owes them something!

ALEA: What?! His life?! Mine?!

RUSTY: There are consequences!

ALEA: There are white consequences, and there are black consequences!

RUSTY: No, sister, you're mixing it up! There are consequences! Period!

ALEA: In your mind! Not mine!

RUSTY: What about Val's?!

ALEA: If they're there, you put them there! Why do you think he took off the handcuffs?! Why do you think he opened the knife?! He knows about consequences! Except he can't live without them! You won't let him!

RUSTY: Val knows what's right!

ALEA: Val knows what works! You know what's right! And now he wants it both ways! That's what's killing him!

RUSTY: And what's he going to think about the next time he arrests somebody?! The next time he throws somebody into a cell?!

ALEA: Nothing! I won't let him! He'll put him in a cell, and then he'll come home!

RUSTY: You don't think there's going to be any remorse?! You don't think he's going to feel anything?!

ALEA: No! No remorse and no consequences! Staying alive, that's our responsibility! Breathing! Functioning! Nothing else matters! Nothing!

RUSTY: I always figured life was a little more complicated than just staying alive!

ALEA: There's nothing more complicated than staying alive!

RUSTY: Then get ready, girl, because you're going to be living with a goddamn stranger!

(Val approaches the platform and stops. Alea notices him and stares at him. Rusty notices him. A silence. Val enters the apartment.)

ALEA: *(To Val)* I called him. I want to get it straight. I want to make sure. I don't want any more "ifs," no more "maybes." I want it clear, absolute, what you're going to tell them tomorrow morning.

VAL: He came at me, three feet, knife out. *(To Rusty)* That's the way it's got to be.

RUSTY: *(Nods)* You got any beer around this place?

(Val nods and turns away)

ALEA: I'll get it. Val?

VAL: I just had one.

(Alea exits)

RUSTY: *(Toward Alea)* No glass. I don't like glasses. *(Trailing off)* Never did. *(To Val)* Wash 'em once, and there's no more "head."

VAL: *(Faces Rusty)* I can't do it. *(Rusty nods)* It won't change anything.

RUSTY: No, it wouldn't. It just depends on who you are.

VAL: Or who you think you should be.

RUSTY: Well, nothing goes according to plan, does it? I accepted that a long time ago.

VAL: Then how come you're disappointed?

RUSTY: I liked the plan. *(Alea reenters with an open can of beer and hands it to Rusty. To Alea)* Thanks. *(He glances at Val— and then Alea. Raises the can)* Cheers.

VAL: Cheers. *(Rusty sips from the beer can. To Rusty)* Do you want a sandwich or something?

RUSTY: No, I'm fine. Too much weight on me. Stallion can't take the corners as fast. Got to keep trim. Cut down on the junk. Two or three beers a day, that's probably too much, but it still doesn't put me over 185. That's my riding weight. I was 195 when I got him. But then I decided to drop ten, and he took off like the wind. It surprised the hell out of me—the difference—ten pounds—what it could do. It surprised the hell out of him, too.

VAL: I've got a wife. I can't take the chance.

RUSTY: I know that, son.

VAL: I've got a job.

RUSTY: I know that, too.

VAL: I don't want to vanish.

RUSTY: Nobody does.

VAL: He was a loser.

RUSTY: Most of them are.

VAL: It was a mistake.

RUSTY: I thought it was an accident.

VAL: It was an accident.

RUSTY: Was it?

VAL: Yes.

RUSTY: I don't buy that, Val. You had him in cuffs.

VAL: Then don't buy it.

RUSTY: I haven't asked for much, son, but I'm asking now. I want an answer. I want the truth. You never have to repeat it. You can lie to your wife. You can lie to your friends. You can lie tomorrow. You can lie for the rest of your goddamn life. But don't lie to me, Val. I want the truth!

ALEA: Why? It won't mean anything. The man's dead.

RUSTY: It'll mean something to me.

ALEA: You're not important! *(Indicates Val)* He is!

RUSTY: I want to hear it once, Val. I want to know if a little bit of me rubbed off on you. Not a lot. Just a little bit. That's all I want to know.

ALEA: *(Turns away)* Goddamn you, Rusty.

RUSTY: You aimed, didn't you?

ALEA: *(Turns back)* Goddamn you!

RUSTY: Didn't you?!

VAL: That's right. I aimed.

ALEA: Of course he did! Didn't you know that?! He probably even toyed with the idea of putting it between the fourth and fifth buttons! That's how good Val is! He wanted to turn it off, just once, and he had the power to do it. He didn't want to hear it anymore. "Nigger." He didn't want the spit in his face. "Nigger!" He wanted to turn it off forever. "NIGGER!" Just like you did, except you never pulled the trigger. You were afraid to do it. So you took it. And took it. And took it! But you tell me—who gave them the right to say it?! And you tell me—why do we have to take it?! It's wrong. He shouldn't have shot him. He should have ignored him. Like you did. But it never would have happened—he never would have even thought about it—if we didn't have to spend most of our lives being tempted to do it! Val had to do it for you! He had to do it for a lot of people like you! Why'd you have to ask?! You couldn't even let him have that, could you? I believed him. The whole story. And I knew it wasn't true. Why'd you have to ask?! *(She turns away from them)*

RUSTY: You can't turn it off, son. I thought you knew that.

VAL: It seemed like a good idea at the time.

RUSTY: I figured it out early. That's why I never pulled the trigger. Everything's temporary. Most people don't stay in your life that long. Not if you're a cop. I thought I taught you that.

VAL: I suppose you did. But I remember you telling me, six years old, the day you found me tied to that tree—"Ain't no differences between a white man and a black man can't be erased by a bullet."

RUSTY: I was angry. What they'd done to you. I didn't mean it.

VAL: You never told me you didn't mean it.

ALEA: *(Turns back)* Rusty? It could have been an accident.

RUSTY: It could have been.

ALEA: Why didn't you just leave it at that?

RUSTY: I was a cop. I got used to answers.

ALEA: It could have been your excuse for not asking him to change his story. It could have been your excuse for not asking him to take a chance on going to jail.

RUSTY: I know. Except I always would have wondered. And that would have been worse.

ALEA: How much worse, Rusty? Don't you think I know what I'm asking him to do? Don't you think I know him? So, what's that make me?

RUSTY: *(Nods—fiddles with his beer can)* Beer's gone. That makes three today. Well, not really . . . It wasn't sixteen ounces. I've got to get up early. Stallion's waiting for me. He's probably short on sugar or something. And it takes a lot longer to drive in New York. I'm trying not to judge you, son . . .

VAL: No, you're not.

RUSTY: I am. But it's hard.

VAL: It's not that hard.

RUSTY: You killed a man. You shot him point-blank. What in the hell do you expect me to do?! Act like it never happened?!

VAL: No, you expect me to pay for it.

RUSTY: I expect it, yes! That's the law!

VAL: Whose law?!

RUSTY: It's the law! It's been around for a long time!

VAL: The law never did shit for us! What's so important about it now?! So why not bend it?! Like they do! When it's convenient! Like you did! When Grandmother needed a fucking television set!

RUSTY: I bent it! You broke it!

VAL: What's the difference?! I don't see it! William H. Willis— a television set?!

RUSTY: TV set don't breathe, that's the difference!

VAL: So that makes it okay, right?!

RUSTY: The sign says "55." I drive "75." We're talking about a cop who aimed!

VAL: No, we're talking about a creep who kept up his patter too long!

RUSTY: He was handcuffed, for Christ's sake!

VAL: What handcuffs? I didn't see any goddamn handcuffs. I just saw his mouth. Then I checked out his heart, and it all made sense. It was making his mouth move. All I had to do was zero in on his heart, and I wouldn't have to watch his mouth move anymore. That's all I saw—his fucking heart! And I wanted to rip it out! And, no, I'm not real certain I want to pay for it. I'm not real sure I want to throw it all away, just for William H. Willis, I'm not! It never happened to you!

RUSTY: I never let it happen!

VAL: And that's why you want me to pay for it!

RUSTY: You lost control, buster! You snapped! That's not why they gave you a badge!

VAL: That's right! I lost it! I finally lost my "cool." I snapped, and it was all out front. And do you want to know how long I've been waiting to do it? All my life! The "chip" just got too heavy, and I didn't want to carry it around anymore. One split second, that's all it took to knock it off, and that made him dead. No, it didn't happen to you. Not you. But let's say it did happen. One time, one night, when you'd finally heard it once too often. It was hot out. It was dark. You were alone. The scum of the earth, spitting it out at you. "Nigger!" "Coon!" "Shine!" "Jigaboo!" And you didn't want to take it anymore. You couldn't take it anymore. And then "click." Nobody heard the shot, and nobody saw him fall. Who was he, anyway? Who in the fuck was he?! What then? What would you have done? Thrown away Mom? Twenty-five years? Thrown away me? Thrown away your friends? Your job? Your reputation? Your weekends on the Allegheny teaching me how to fish? Your nights in the Poconos—after supper—teaching me how to ride? Is that what you would have done, Rusty? Just because some son of a bitch, the lowest of the low, finally screamed "nigger" at you once too often and once too loud?! Is it?!

(Rusty fiddles with his beer can)

RUSTY: I'd like to think—I'd like to think I would have assumed the responsibility. That's what I'd like to think.

ALEA: Which one?

RUSTY: The more important one.

ALEA: Which one, Rusty?

VAL: He would have gone to jail.

Dennis McIntyre

ALEA: Is that what you would have done? Is it?

RUSTY: I think so, yes.

VAL: I could kill you for saying that!

RUSTY: I doubt it!

VAL: Mom, me— No, I could do it!

RUSTY: How?! I'm not cuffed! *(Val and Rusty glare at each other. Alea turns away from them. Val turns away from Rusty)* I didn't mean that, son.

VAL: *(Faces him)* Neither did I.

(Rusty sets his beer can down. He moves to exit. He stops. He faces them. Alea faces Rusty)

RUSTY: I'll be in the country, you maybe need me. Spence's place again. You've got the number. I think—I think I'm going to look at some land. I'd like to have a little land. I could maybe build me a permanent stable— *(Shakes his head "no")* There I go again. It'd probably blow over—the first winter storm . . . *(Rusty starts to exit again. He stops.)* If I could— If there was any way, Val—If I were still in uniform—If I could convince anyone—I'd take credit for the guy you shot. I'd claim it. I would. I'd make it mine.

VAL: I know. *(Rusty begins to exit again)* Rusty? *(Rusty stops.)* You—You keep in touch, okay?

RUSTY: Sure, son. I'll try to do that. *(Rusty and Val stare at each other)* You know, the funny thing, I moved out of Pittsburgh to get closer to you.

(Rusty exits. Alea moves to Val)

82

ALEA: He's old, Val. We can't listen to him. *(No response from Val)* We can't afford to listen to him. *(No response from Val)* We've got a life. *(No response from Val. Voice breaking)* Val?

(The lights slowly fade to darkness. Sound—immediately—voices —indistinct)

Scene 5

(Sounds out—gradually—the voices. Lights—another platform. The next morning. Val, a minimum change of clothes, sits in a witness chair)

VAL: *(Without looking up)* I spotted said perpetrator, William H. Willis, at approximately 11:15, on the evening of July Fourth. Suspect was in the process of committing grand theft auto—a tan, 1977 Oldsmobile, license number "817 Y as in yellow, V as in victor, C as in Charlie," parked on West Twenty-seventh Street and Tenth Avenue. I approached the suspect, identifying myself as a police officer. Suspect immediately fled north on Tenth Avenue, turning west on West Twenty-eighth Street. I pursued the suspect on foot, catching up with him approximately six minutes later on the south side of the 500 block of West Twenty-eighth Street. I drew my service revolver and ordered the suspect to halt. Suspect— Suspect came to a halt between—West Twenty-eighth Street —and—Eleventh Avenue—I approached the suspect—I approached the suspect—and ordered—I—ordered him to—I called for "transportation"—

PARKER'S VOICE: Officer Johnson? Could you please speak up? And could you also look up, please? We can't see your face.

(Val grips his legs and squeezes them)

VAL: *(Without looking up)* I approached the suspect—William H. Willis—and I—I—I ordered him to— Suspect—

85

PARKER'S VOICE: Officer Johnson, please? We can't hear you, and we can't see your face. *(Val grips his legs harder. He doesn't look up)* Officer Johnson? *(Val slowly relaxes his hands. He looks up slowly and stares straight ahead)* Thank you, Officer Johnson. That's much better. Please continue.

VAL: I called "transportation." I approached the suspect with the specific intention of patting him down and placing him in handcuffs. When I was within three feet of him, the suspect turned on me with an open knife in his right hand. I backed up two feet and ordered the suspect to drop the knife. The suspect did not comply with my order, but instead, made a menacing movement in my direction, the knife still in his hand. I fired my service revolver once, the bullet striking the suspect in the chest and killing him instantly.

(The lights slowly begin to fade on Val. He remains motionless. He stares straight ahead. The life seems to have gone out of him. Music. Blackout. The music plays in the darkness. Music out)

THE END